WHERE THE WILD DADS WENT

For Jon, and my dad – two of the best wild things around!
K. B.

To my father, forever and always a Wild Dad.
S. W.

First published in the UK in 2016
First published in the US in 2017
by Faber and Faber Limited
Bloomsbury House,
74–77 Great Russell Street, London WC1B 3DA

ISBN 978-0-571-33211-3

Printed in Malta

3 5 7 9 10 8 6 4 2

The moral rights of Katie Blackburn and Sholto Walker have been asserted.
A CIP record for this book is available from the British Library.

WHERE THE WILD DADS WENT

Written by
KATIE BLACKBURN

Illustrated by
SHOLTO WALKER

The night Dad had a few cheeky ones after work,
forgot the milk he was supposed to fetch,

and tripped over the rubbish,

Mum called him A Wild Thing

and said "Don't mind *me*!" and spent the rest of the evening
on the phone with Debs from down the road.

As Dad skulked on the sofa, a distant drumbeat began to pound and wild shadows chased across the floor.

A jungle grew up out of the carpet thick and strong

And Dad grabbed a vine and climbed
and climbed,

through the years,

and over continents,

until he came to the land
where the Wild Dads are.

And then he roared!

And the Wild Dads heard that roar, and they pumped their manly fists, and they raised their manly drinks,

but Dad laughed and played air guitar like the rock god that he really was

and they were secretly impressed and said he should be
King of the Wild Dads. And Dad agreed.

'Now, let's get on it!' Dad roared.

And there was never a rumpus like it.

Until –
'Woaah, time out!' Dad moaned. For the King of the Wild Dads suddenly felt a bit tired and emotional. And then he remembered a place where he was safe from trouble.

And all at once he wished he was with those he loved more than anything in the world. Though miles away, Dad sensed that he was missed.

So he stopped being
King of the Wild Dads.

'You cannot go,' the Wild
Dads wailed, 'we're going
clubbing!' But Dad
said, 'No.'

And sobbing manly tears,
they punched each other's
arms, and bear hugged
manfully, and

Dad took hold of a vine and swung through the years and over continents

until he was back in his very own front room.

Someone had put a blanket
over him.

And there was a cup of tea
and a beaker of water.

It was all right.
He was home.